AUTHENTIC TRANSCRIPTIONS
WITH NOTES AND TABLATURE

Music transcriptions by Ron Piccione

ISBN 978-1-4234-0417-0

CORPORATION

7777 W. BLUEMOUND RD. P.O. BOX 13819 MILWAUKEE, WI 53213

Visit Hal Leonard Online at
www.halleonard.com

Detroit Rock City

Words and Music by Paul Stanley and Bob Ezrin

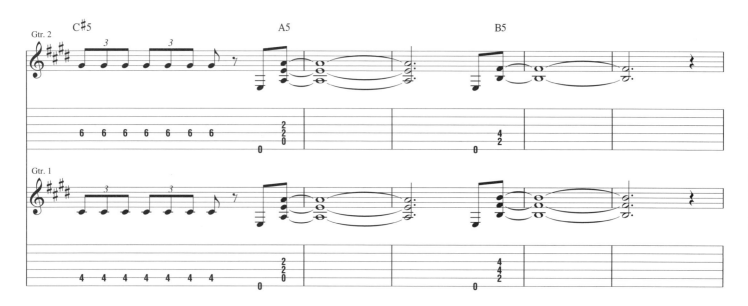

*Paul Stanley
**Chord symbols reflect implied harmony.

***Ace Frehley (w/ Les Paul style electronics; set
lead volume to 10 and rhythm volume to 0).

2nd time, Gtr. 1: w/ Rhy. Fill 1

B5   F#5   C#5

ra - di - o's the on - ly light._____ I hear my song, it pulls me through.___
know I got - ta hit the road._____ First I drink, then I smoke.
still mov - in' much too slow._____ I feel so good, so a - live. I'm so___

End Rhy. Fig. 3

2nd & 3rd times, Gtr. 2: w/ Rhy. Fill 2

E5   B5   F#5

It comes on strong, tells me what I got - ta do._____ I got ___
Start the car, try to make the mid - night show._____ Let's
____ a - live. I hear my song play - in' on the ra - di - o._____ It goes... ___

End Rhy. Fig. 4

End Rhy. Fig. 2

Rhy. Fill 1

Gtr. 1

fdbk.

Pitch: F

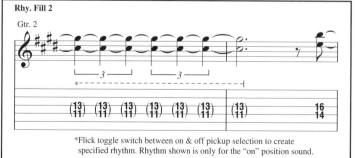

Rhy. Fill 2

Gtr. 2

*Flick toggle switch between on & off pickup selection to create
specified rhythm. Rhythm shown is only for the "on" position sound.

Chorus

2nd time, Gtr. 1: w/ Rhy. Fill 3
3rd time, Gtr. 1: w/ Rhy. Fill 4

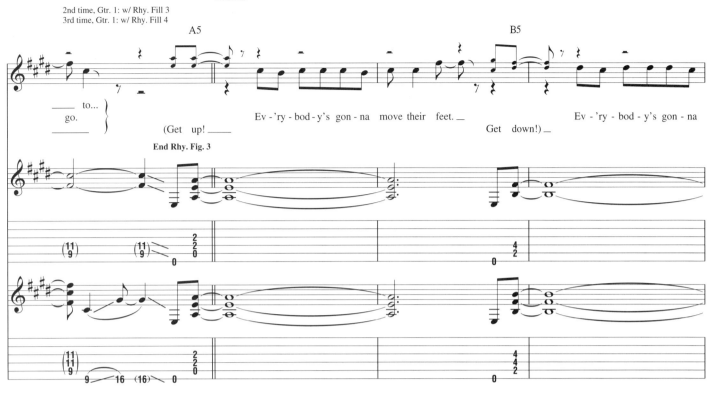

Ev - 'ry - bod - y's gon - na move their feet. __ Ev - 'ry - bod - y's gon - na

(Get up! __ Get down!) __

End Rhy. Fig. 3

leave their seat. __ You got - ta lose your mind in De - troit Rock

Rhy. Fill 3

Gtr. 1

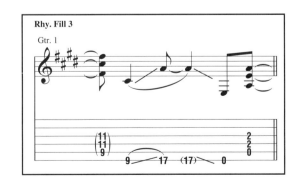

Rhy. Fill 4

Gtr. 1

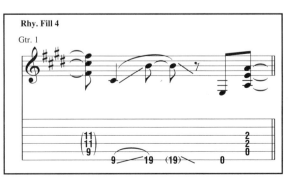

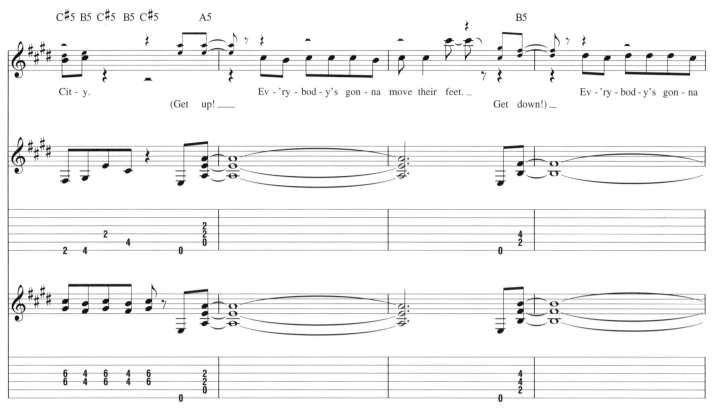

⊕ Coda 1

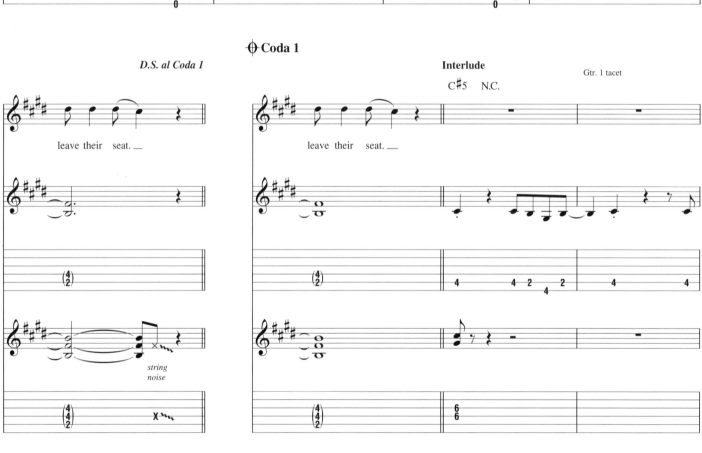

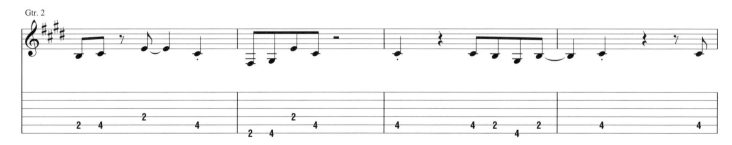

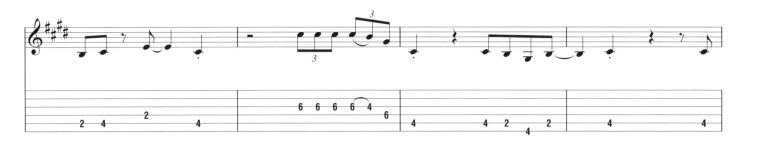

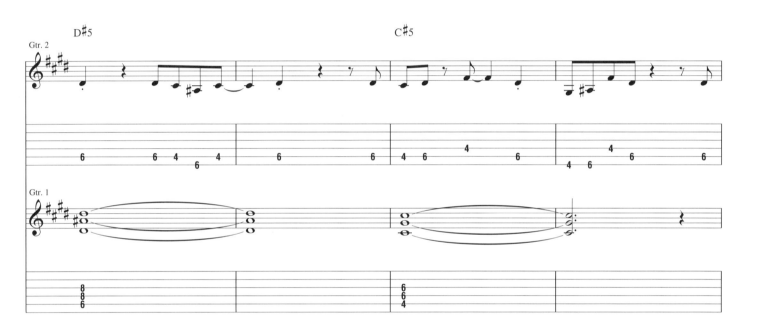

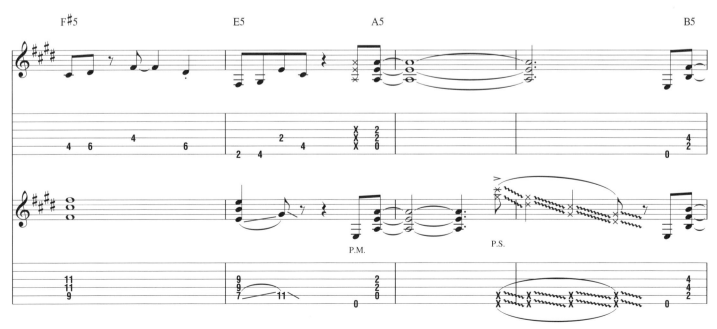

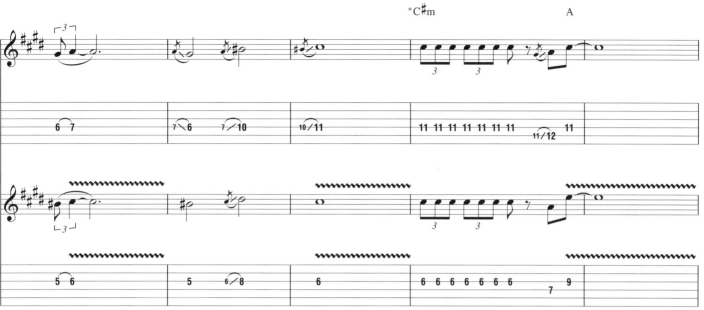

*Chords implied by bass, next 13 meas.

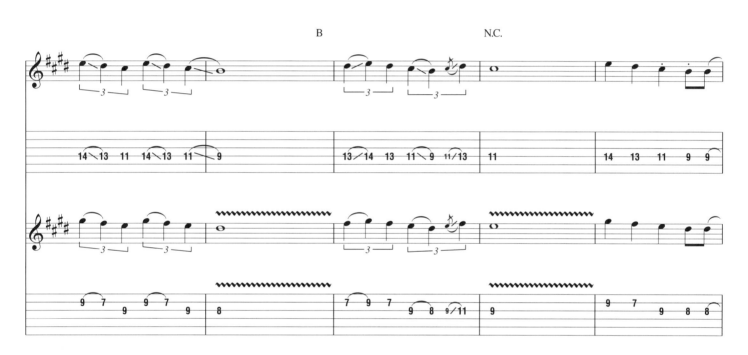

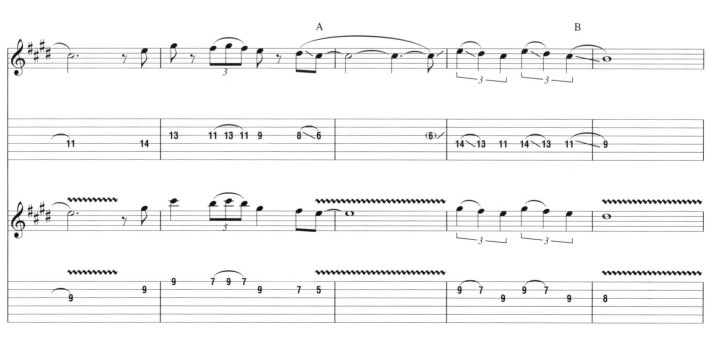

Verse

4. Twelve o'-clock, __ I got-ta, got-ta rock. __ There's a __ truck a-head, lights star-in' at my eyes. __ Oh, my God, __ no time to turn. __ I got to laugh, __ I know I'm gon-na die. __ Why? __

Outro-Chorus

Ev-'ry-bod-y's gon-na move their feet. __

Pitch: F

Gtr. 1: w/ Rhy. Fig. 2
Gtr. 2: w/ Rhy. Fig. 3

Gtr. 2: w/ Rhy. Fill 2

Gtr. 2: w/ Rhy. Fig. 4

Gtr. 1: w/ Rhy. Fill 4

(Get up!) __

Gtr. 2

Gtr. 1

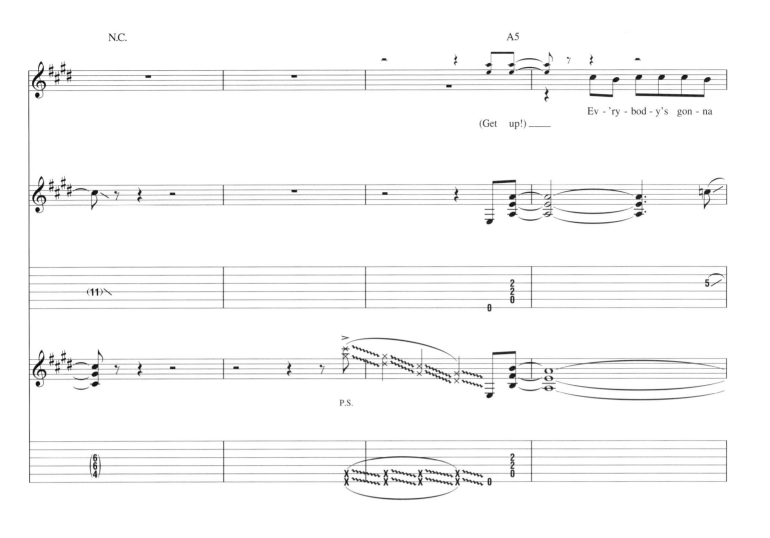

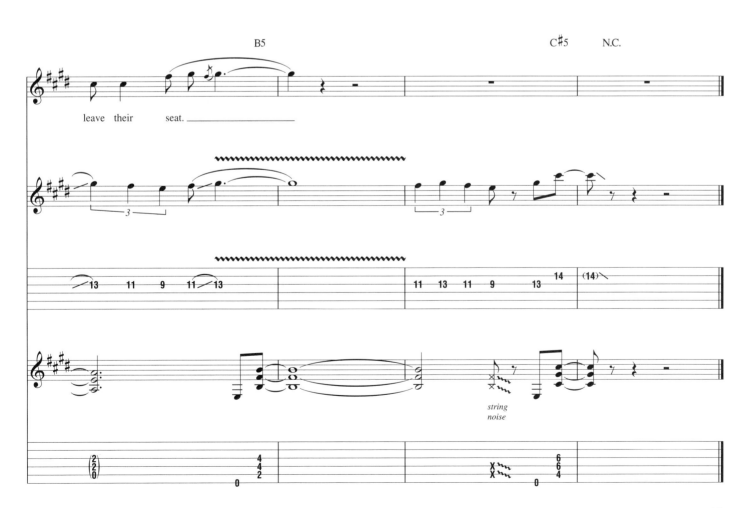

King of the Night Time World

Words and Music by Paul Stanley, Bob Ezrin, Kim Fowley and Mark Anthony

Tune down 1/2 step:
(low to high) Eb-Ab-Db-Gb-Bb-Eb

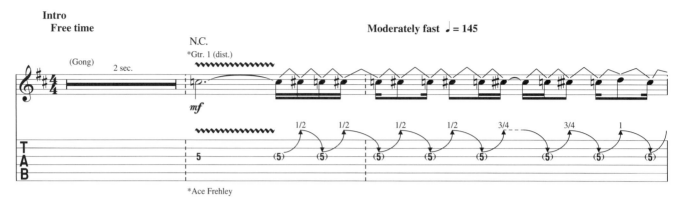

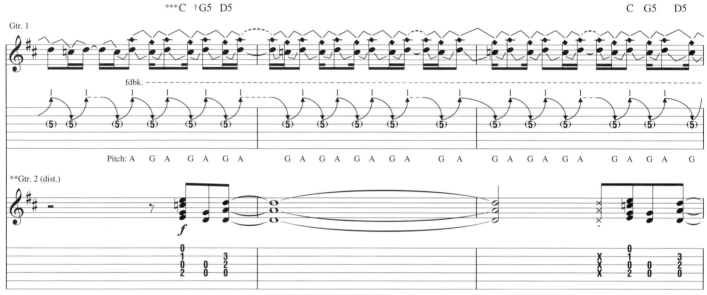

Paul Stanley* ***Chord symbols reflect implied harmony.*
†Bass plays G on all G5 chords throughout.

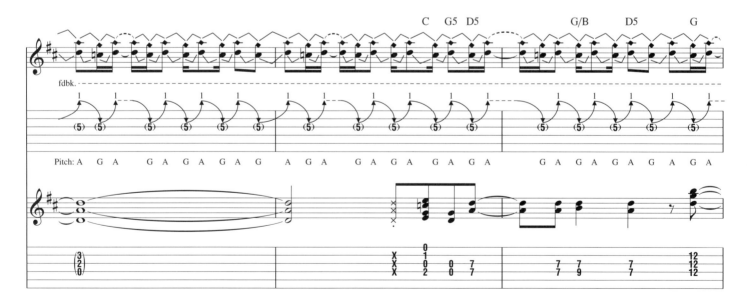

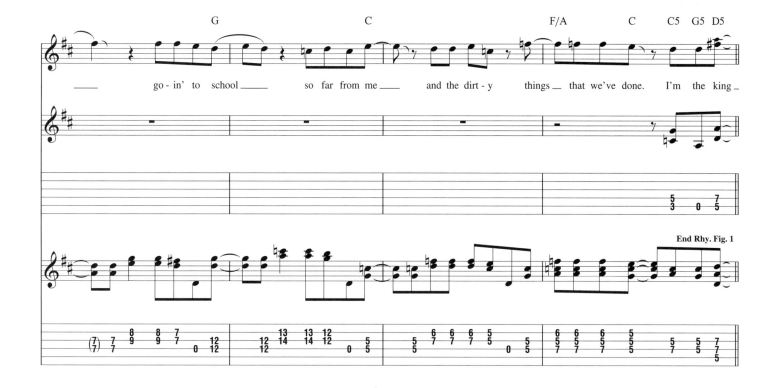

go-in' to school _____ so far from me _____ and the dirt-y things _ that we've done. I'm the king _

End Rhy. Fig. 1

𝄋 Chorus

2nd time, Gtr. 1: w/ Rhy. Fill 1

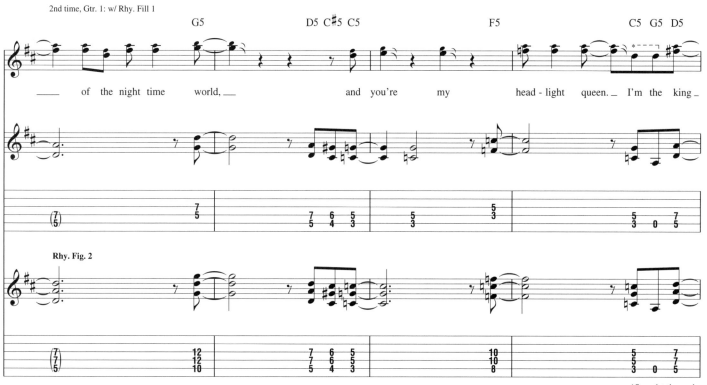

_____ of the night time world, _____ and you're my head-light queen. _ I'm the king _

Rhy. Fig. 2

*Sung 1st time only.

Rhy. Fill 1

Gtr. 1

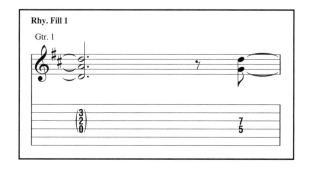

se - cret dream. __ Al - right. __

w/ Lead Voc. ad lib.

D5

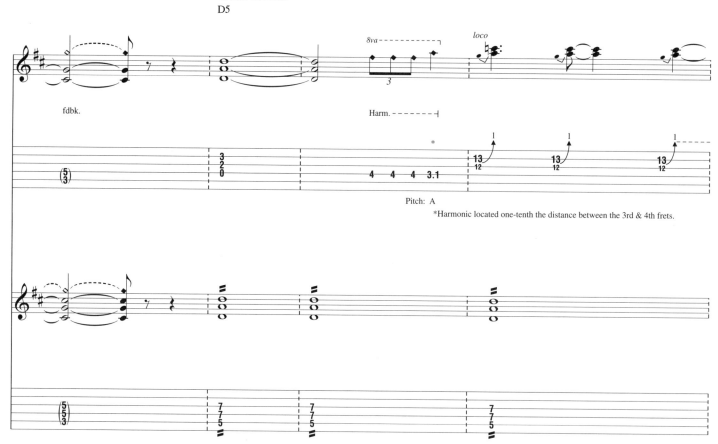

Pitch: A

*Harmonic located one-tenth the distance between the 3rd & 4th frets.

N.C.

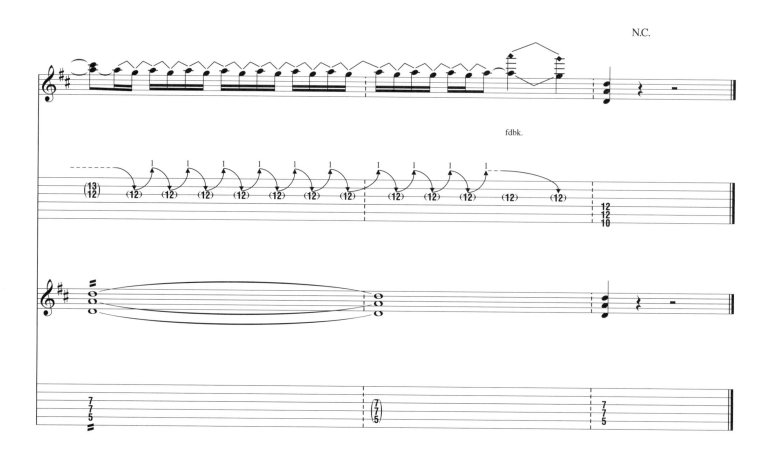

Ladies Room

Words and Music by Gene Simmons

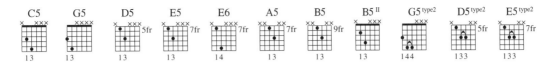

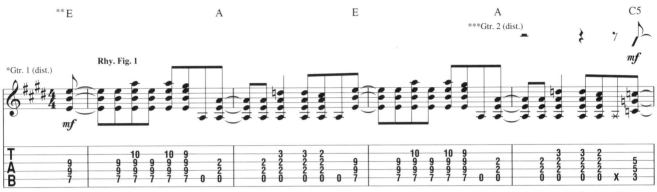

Tune down 1/2 step:
(low to high) E♭-A♭-D♭-G♭-B♭-E♭

Intro
Moderately fast ♩ = 142

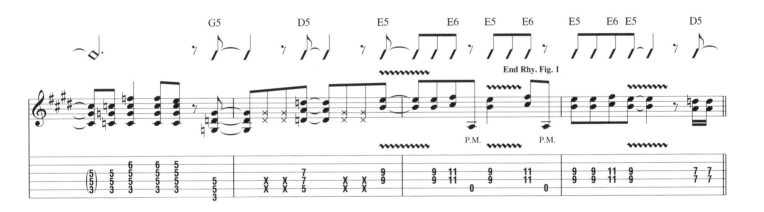

*Paul Stanley **Chord symbols reflect basic harmony.

***Ace Frehley (w/ Les Paul style electronics, set lead volume to 10 and rhythm volume to 0).

Verse

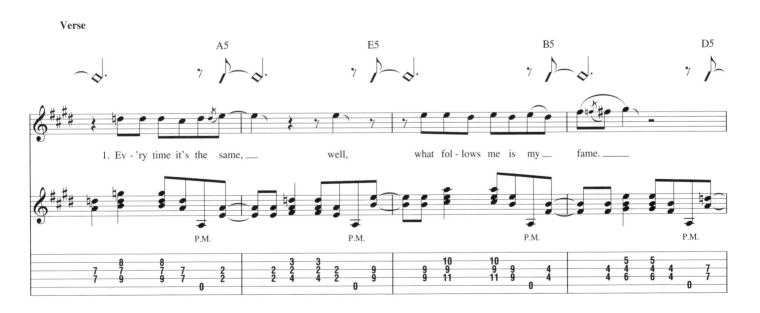

1. Ev-'ry time it's the same, ___ well, what fol-lows me is my ___ fame. ___

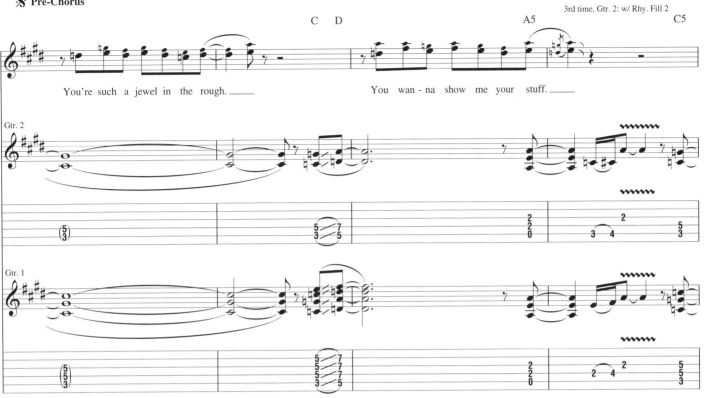

You're such a jewel in the rough. _____ You wan - na show me your stuff. _____

For my mon - ey, you can't be too soon. _____ No!

*Sung 1st & 2nd times only.

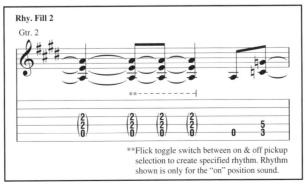

Rhy. Fill 2

Gtr. 2

**Flick toggle switch between on & off pickup selection to create specified rhythm. Rhythm shown is only for the "on" position sound.

Makin' Love

Words and Music by Paul Stanley and Sean Delaney

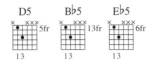

Gtr. 1: Tune down 1/2 step, capo I:
(low to high) Eb-Ab-Db-Gb-Bb-Eb
Gtr. 2: Tune down 1/2 step:
(low to high) Eb-Ab-Db-Gb-Bb-Eb

Intro
Free time

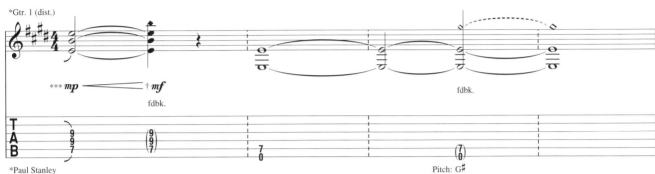

*Paul Stanley
**Symbols in parentheses represent chord names respective to capoed guitar.
Symbols above reflect actual sounding chords. Capoed fret is "0" in tab.
***Vol. swell   †Full vol.

Fast ♩ = 168

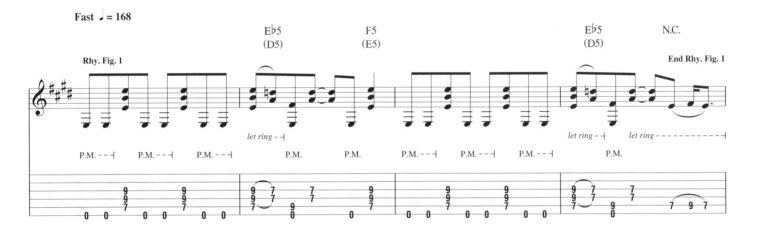

Yea.

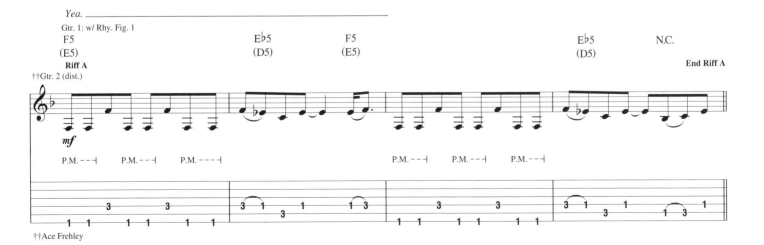

††Ace Frehley

Love Gun

Words and Music by Paul Stanley

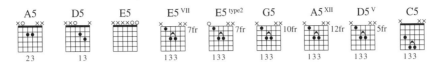

Tune down 1/2 step:
(low to high) Eb-Ab-Db-Gb-Bb-Eb

Intro
Moderately fast ♩ = 153

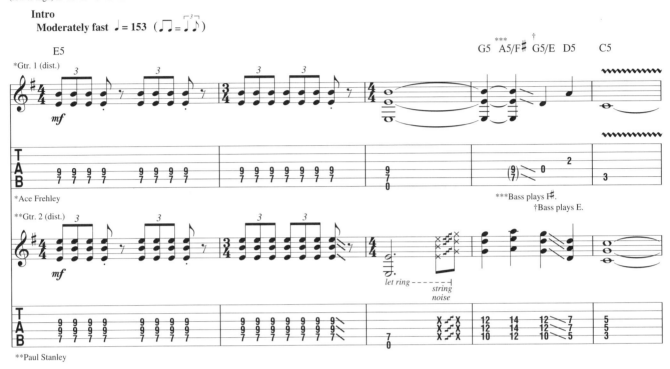

*Ace Frehley
**Gtr. 2 (dist.)
**Paul Stanley

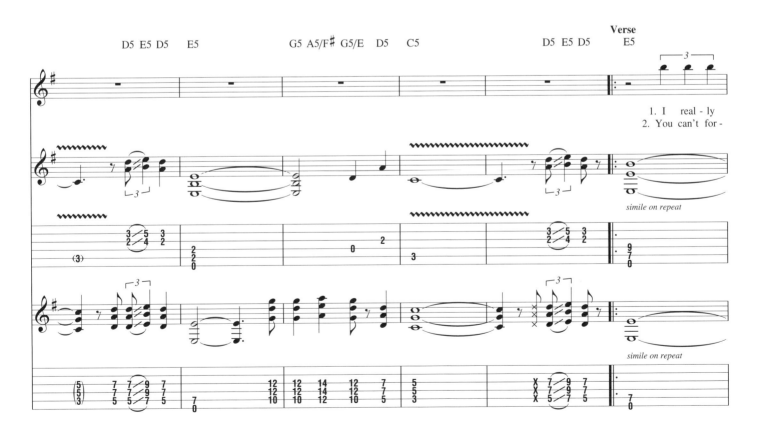

Interlude

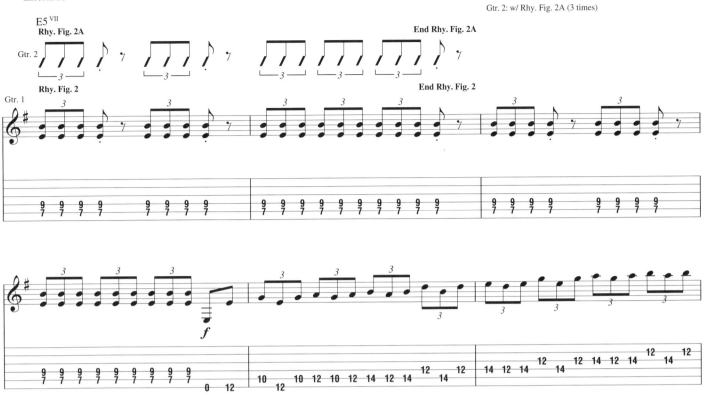

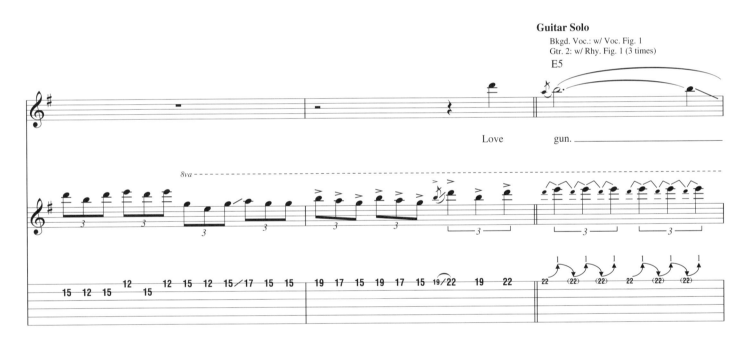

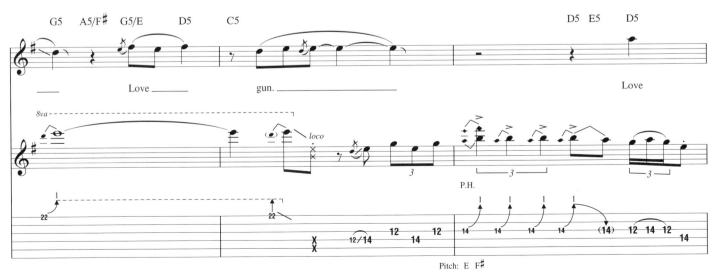

Calling Dr. Love

Words and Music by Gene Simmons

Tune down 1/2 step:
(low to high) E♭-A♭-D♭-G♭-B♭-E♭

Intro

Moderately fast ♩ = 136

*Gtr. 1 (dist.)

Rhy. Fig. 1

*Ace Frehley

Gtr. 1

Rhy. Fig. 2

End Rhy. Fig. 2

**Gtr. 2 (dist.)

**Paul Stanley

Gtr. 1: w/ Rhy. Fig. 2

Verse

Gtr. 1: w/ Rhy. Fig. 2 (1 1/4 times)

1. You need my love, ba - by,

Gtr. 2

Rhy. Fig. 3

End Rhy. Fig. 3

Rhy. Fig. 4

oh, so bad. ___ You're not the on - ly one I've ev - er had. ___ And you say you wan - na

set me free. Don't you know you'll be in mis - er - y. ___ You know ___ why? ___ They

Chorus

call me, ___ they call me Doc - tor Love. ___

(Doc - tor Love. ___ Call - ing Doc - tor Love. ___

Guitar Solo

Christine Sixteen

Words and Music by Gene Simmons

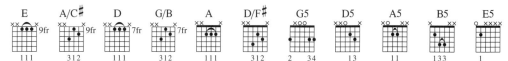

Tune down 1/2 step:
(low to high) Eb-Ab-Db-Gb-Bb-Eb

Intro

Moderately fast ♩ = 134

N.C.(E)

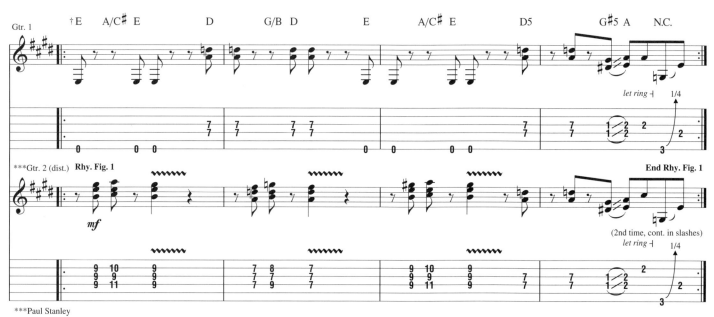

*Gtr. 1 (dist.)

*Ace Frehley (w/ Les Paul style electronics, set
lead volume to 10 and rhythm volume to 0.)

**Play with slight P.M. when recalled as Riff A.

***Paul Stanley

†Chord symbols reflect combined harmony.

𝄋 **Verse**

1. She's got me diz - zy, _____ she sees me through to the end. _____ Oo,
2. She drives me cra - zy, ____ I want to give her what I've got. ____ Oo,

Shock Me

Words and Music by Ace Frehley

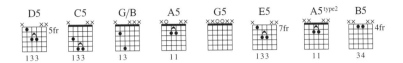

Tune down 1/2 step:
(low to high) E♭-A♭-D♭-G♭-B♭-E♭

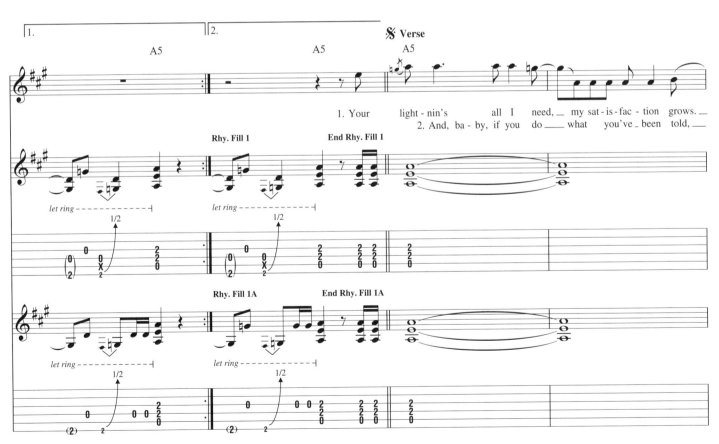

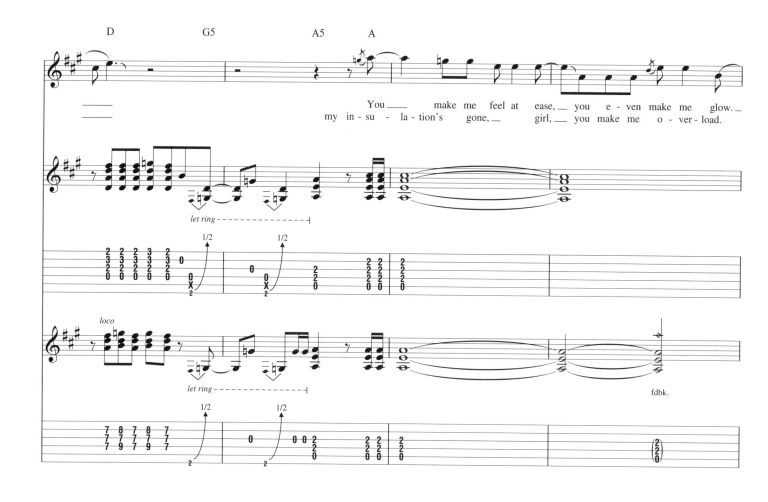

You__ make me feel at ease,__ you e - ven make me glow.__
my in - su - la - tion's gone,__ girl,__ you make me o - ver - load.

Pre-Chorus

Don't cut the pow - er on me. I'm feel - in'
Don't pull the plug on__ me,__ no, no. Keep it in,__

(cont. in slashes)

Chorus
D5 C5 G/B A5 G5 D5
Rhy. Fig. 2A
Gtr. 2
low, so get me high.
and keep me high.
Shock me.
(Make me feel bet-ter.
Gtr. 1
Rhy. Fig. 2
C5 A5 G5 D5 C5
End Rhy. Fig. 2A
Shock me.
Put on your black leath-er.
End Rhy. Fig. 2
To Coda
A5 G5 D5 E5
Shock me.
We can come to-geth-er.)
Interlude
D.S. al Coda
Gtrs. 1 & 2: w/ Rhy. Figs. 1 & 1A
D/A A D/A A D/A A G5 D G5 A5
Gtrs. 1 & 2: w/ Rhy. Fills 1 & 1A

$\oplus$ **Coda**

C' - mon.

(cont. in notation)

Guitar Solo

D   **G5**   **A5**   **D/A A**   **D/A A**

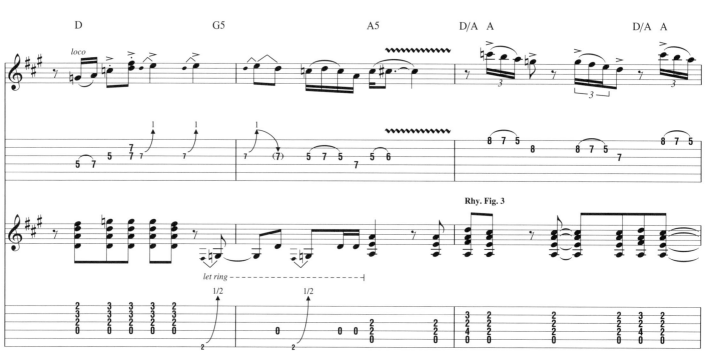

Rhy. Fig. 3

Guitar Solo

Free time

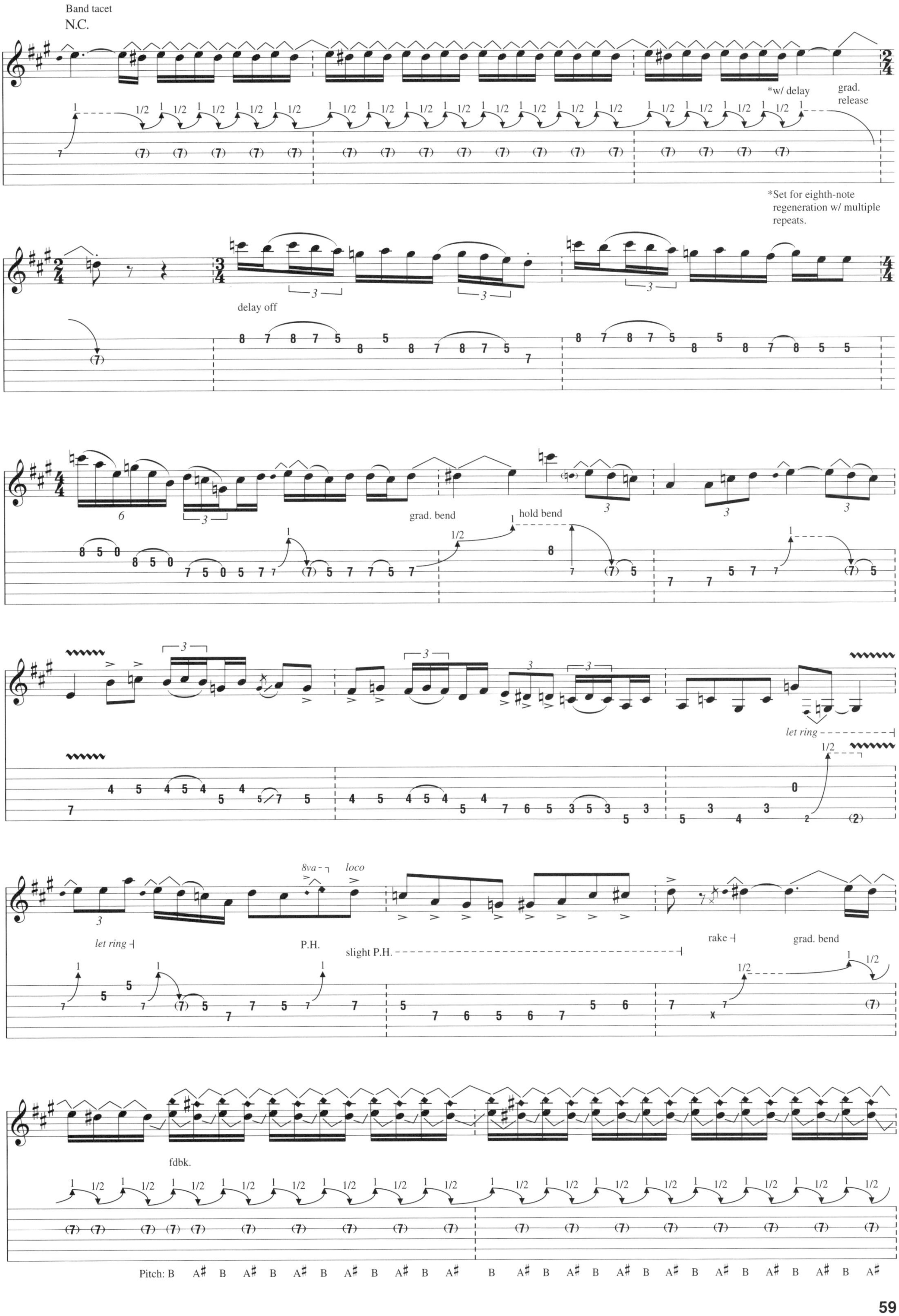

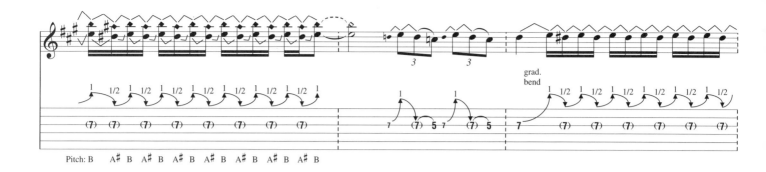

Pitch: B A♯ B A♯ B A♯ B A♯ B A♯ B A♯ B

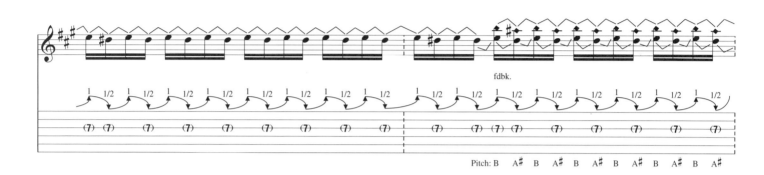

Pitch: B A♯ B A♯ B A♯ B A♯ B A♯ B A♯

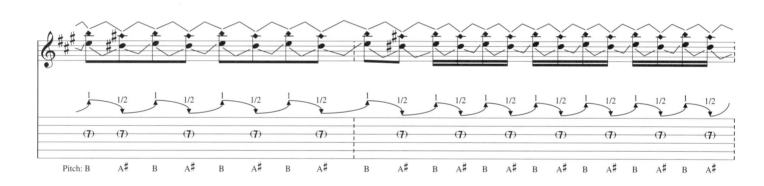

Pitch: B A♯ B A♯ B A♯ B A♯   B A♯ B A♯ B A♯ B A♯ B A♯ B A♯

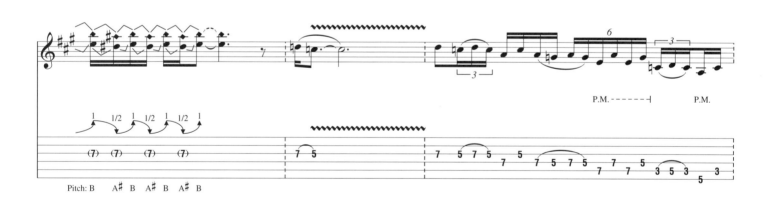

Pitch: B A♯ B A♯ B A♯ B

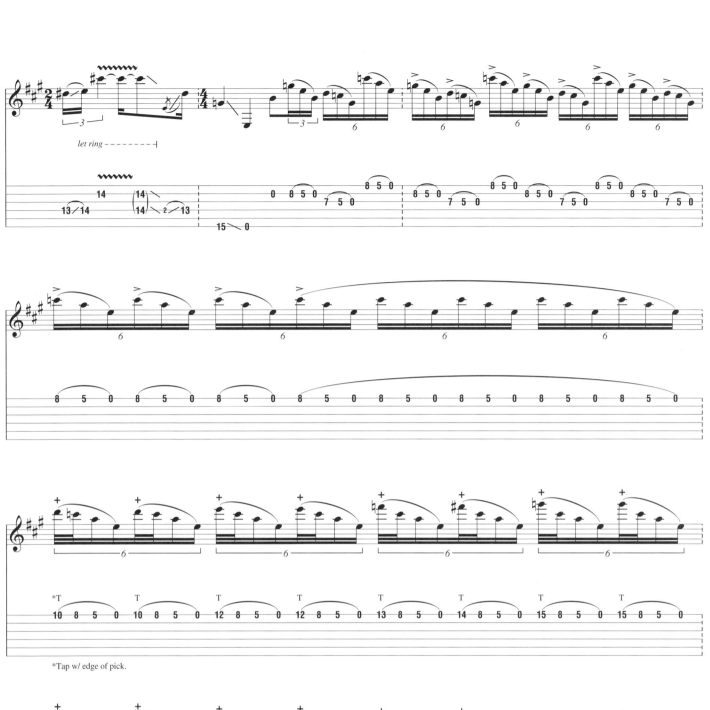

*Tap w/ edge of pick.

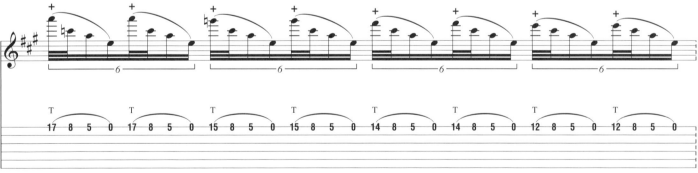

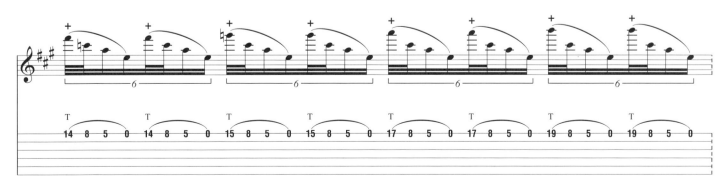

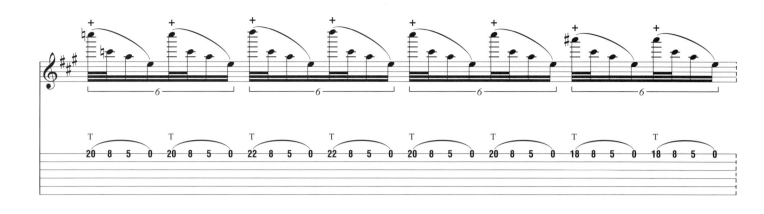

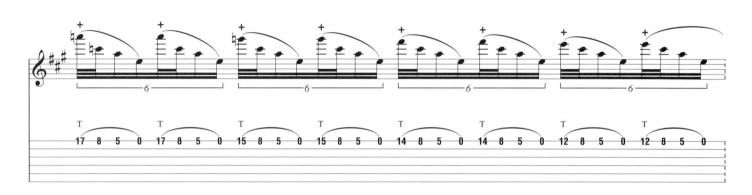

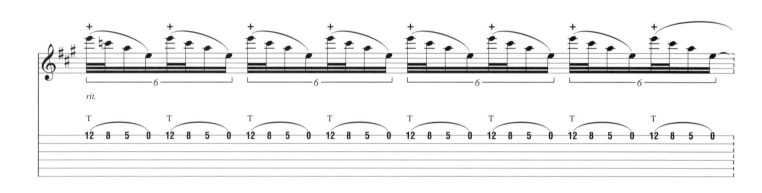

Outro
w/ Lead Voc. ad lib.

A5

N.C.

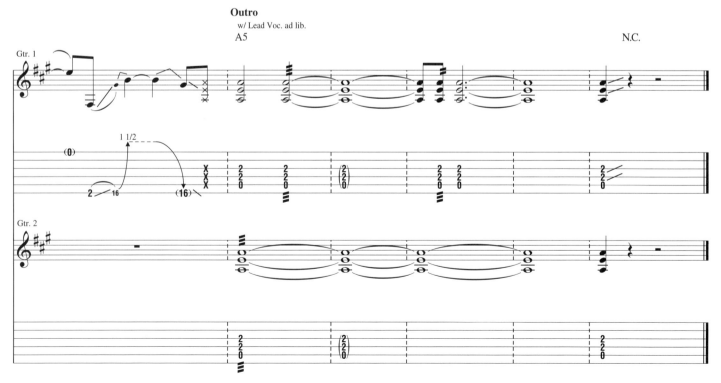

Hard Luck Woman

Words and Music by Paul Stanley

Tune down 1/2 step:
(low to high) Eb-Ab-Db-Gb-Bb-Eb

†Substitute note in parenthesis when Riff A is recalled 1st time only.

hard luck wom-an.____ Rags,_____ the sail-or's on-ly daugh-ter. A

child ____ of ____ the wa-ter. Too proud to be ____ a ____ queen.____
(Proud to be ____ a ____ queen.) __

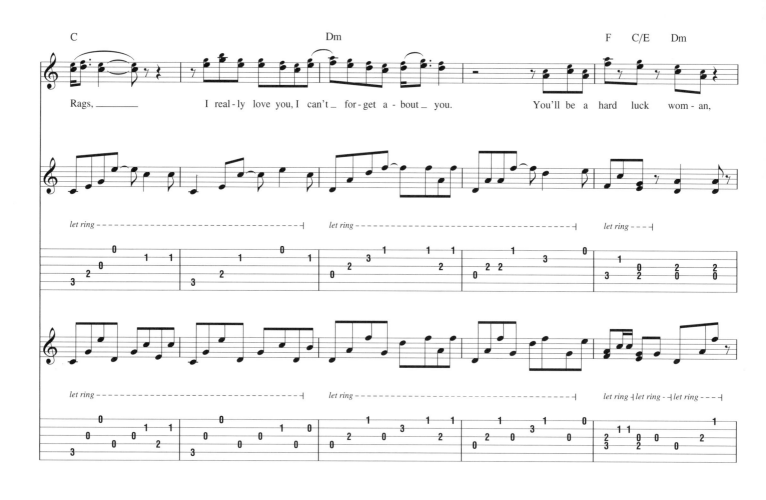

Rags, _____ I real-ly love you, I can't __ for-get a - bout __ you. You'll be a hard luck wom - an,

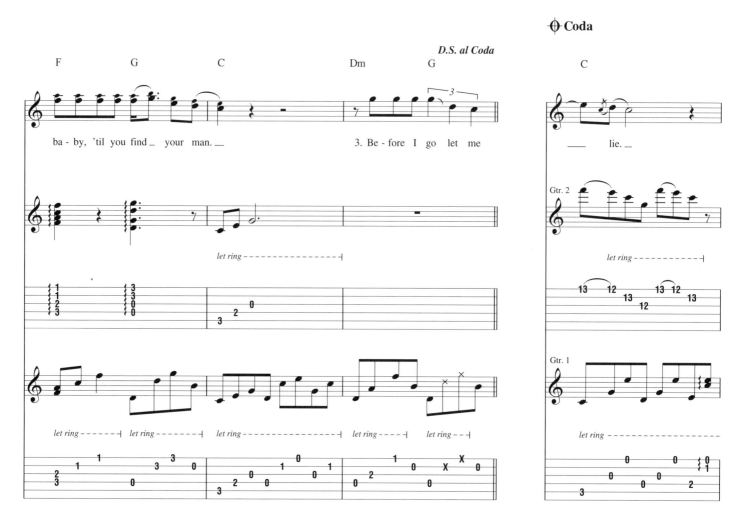

ba - by, 'til you find __ your man. __ 3. Be - fore I go let me _____ lie. __

Pre-Chorus

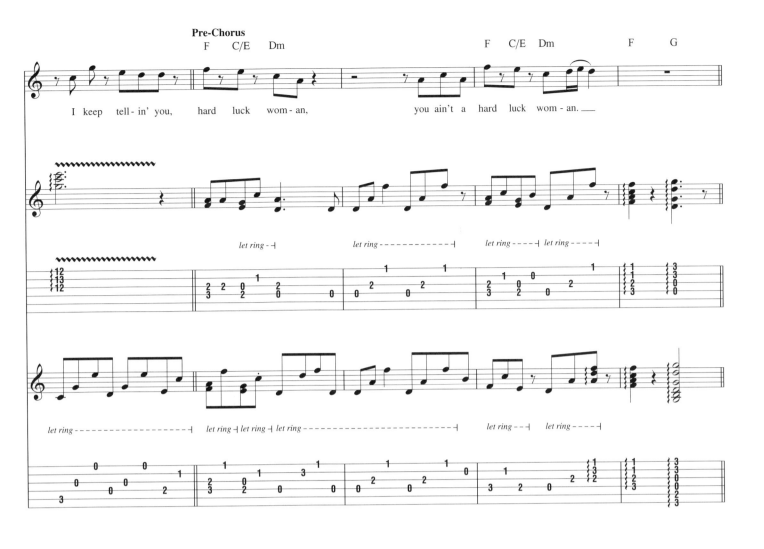

I keep tell-in' you, hard luck wom-an, you ain't a hard luck wom-an.

Chorus

Rags,_____ the sail-or's on - ly daugh - ter. A child __ of __ the wa - ter. Too

proud   to   be __ a __   queen. ____   Rags, _____   I real-ly love you, I can't __
(Proud to   be __ a __   queen.) _

for - get a - bout __ you.   You'll be a hard luck wom - an,   ba - by, 'til you find __ your man. __

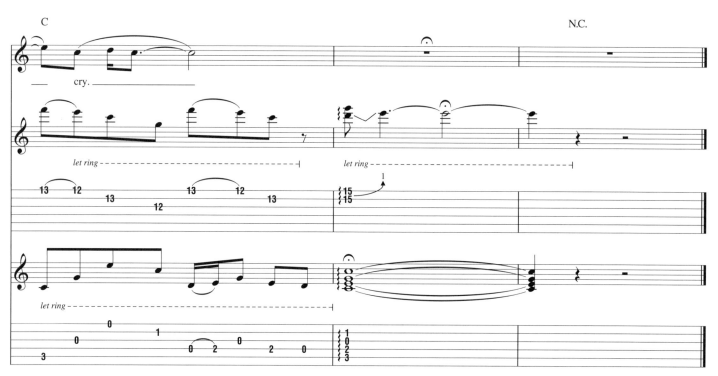

Tomorrow and Tonight

Words and Music by Paul Stanley

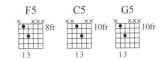

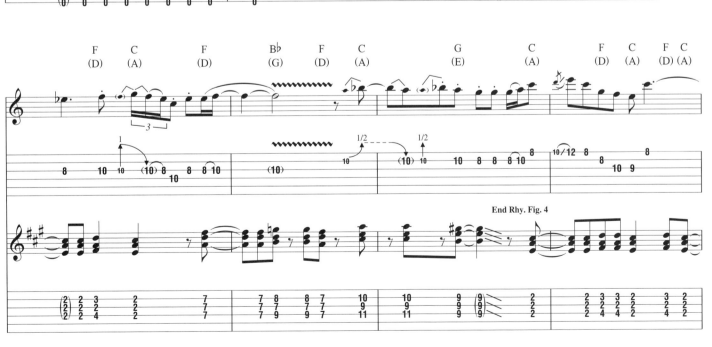

Chorus

*Refers to upstemmed voc. only

I Stole Your Love

Words and Music by Paul Stanley

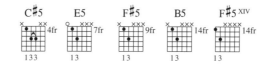

Tune down 1/2 step:
(low to high) Eb-Ab-Db-Gb-Bb-Eb

*Paul Stanley
**Ace Frehley

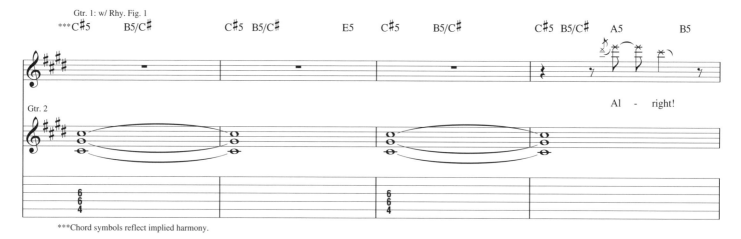

***Chord symbols reflect implied harmony.

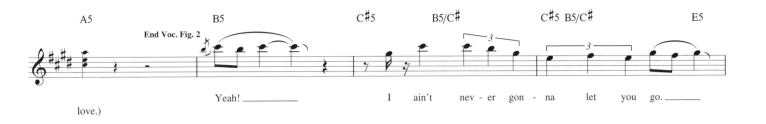

Yeah! _____ I ain't nev - er gon - na let you go. _____
love.)

I, _____ I stole _ your love, _____

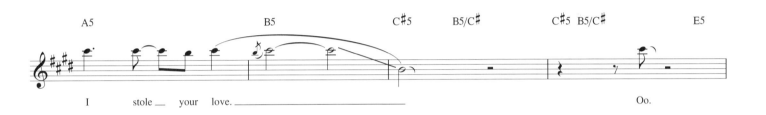

I stole _ your love. _____ Oo.

I stole _ your _ love, I stole _ your _ love,

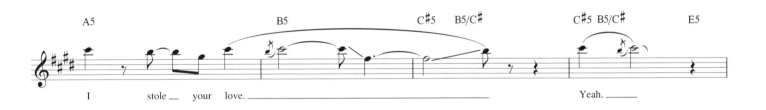

I stole _ your love. _____ Yeah. _____

I, _____ I stole _ your love, _____

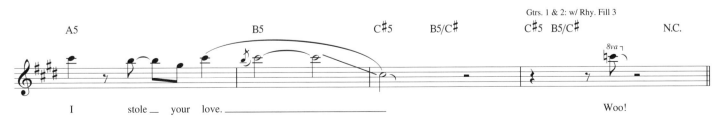

I stole _ your love. _____ Woo!

Beth

Words and Music by Bob Ezrin, Stanley Penridge and Peter Criss

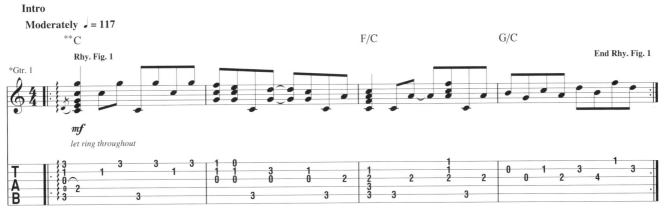

*Composite of piano & orchestra arr. for gtr.
**Chord symbols reflect basic harmony.

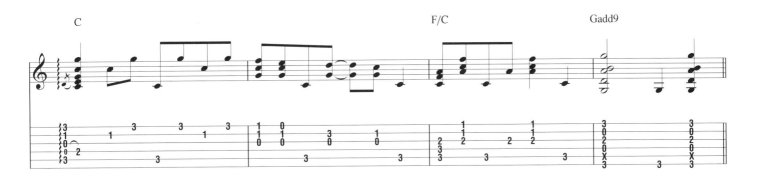

1. Beth, I hear you call-ing, but I can't come home right now. ___
2. You say you feel so emp-ty, that our house just ain't a home. ___

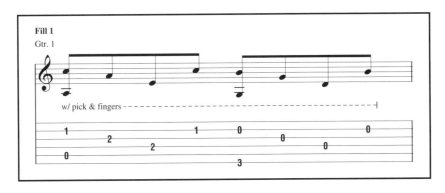

Verse

3. Beth, __ you __ say you're lone - ly and I _____ hope you'll __ be al - right, __

'cause me and the boys __ will be play - in' all

Outro

Gtr. 1: w/ Rhy. Fig. 1 (1 1/2 times)

night, _____ ah. _____

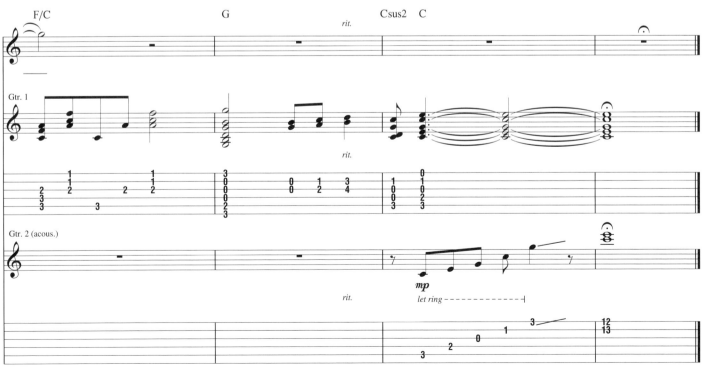

Gtr. 1

Gtr. 2 (acous.)

God of Thunder

Words and Music by Paul Stanley

Tune down 1/2 step:
(low to high) Eb-Ab-Db-Gb-Bb-Eb

Intro
Moderately ♩ = 120

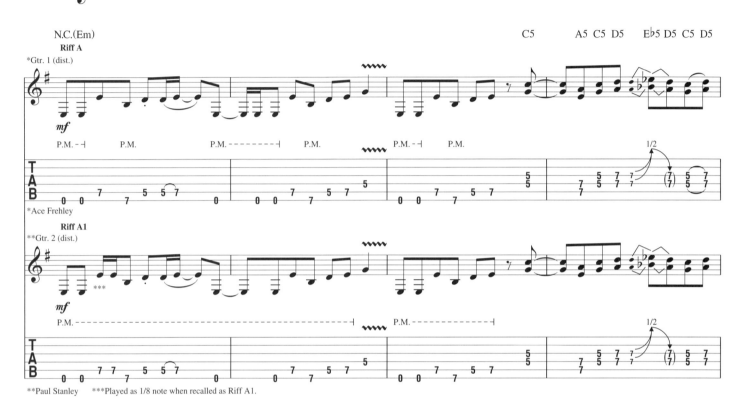

*Gtr. 1 (dist.)

*Ace Frehley

**Paul Stanley   ***Played as 1/8 note when recalled as Riff A1.

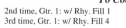

C5   G   D5   E5   C5 B5 C5 B5 C5 G5 D5

The spell you're un - der   will slow - ly rob you of your virg - in soul. ___
                                                                          (Soul.) __

Interlude

Gtrs. 1 & 2: w/ Riffs A & A1 (1st 4 meas.)

Guitar Solo

Gtr. 2: w/ Riff A1 (1st 4 meas., 2 1/2 times)

N.C.(Em)   C5   A5 C5 D5 Eb5 D5 C5 D5

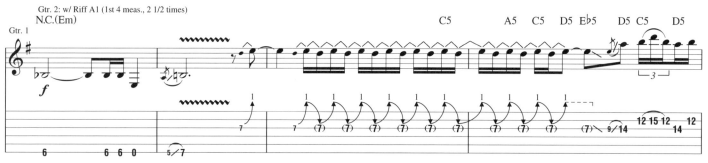

N.C.(Em)   C5

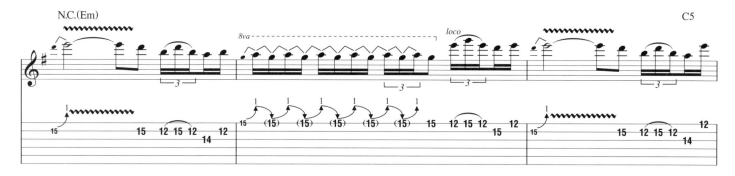

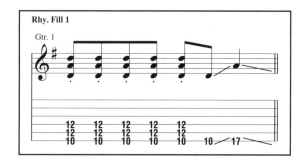

Rhy. Fill 1
Gtr. 1

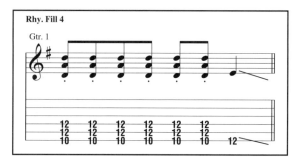

Rhy. Fill 4
Gtr. 1

I Want You

Words and Music by Paul Stanley

Tune down 1/2 step:
(low to high) E♭-A♭-D♭-G♭-B♭-E♭

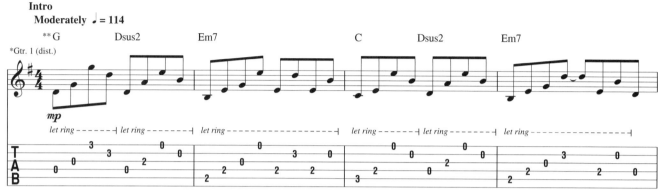

*Paul Stanley (w/ vol. control set to 1/2 volume).
**Chord symbols reflect implied harmony.

***Ace Frehley

†Full vol.

Chorus

*Refers to upstemmed vocals only.

Verse

*T = Thumb on 6th string

**Decrease to 1/2 vol.

Bridge

Faster ♩ = 110

In the morn-in' I raise __ my head __ and I'm think-in' of days __ gone __ by. __ And the

Shout It Out Loud

Words and Music by Paul Stanley, Gene Simmons and Bob Ezrin

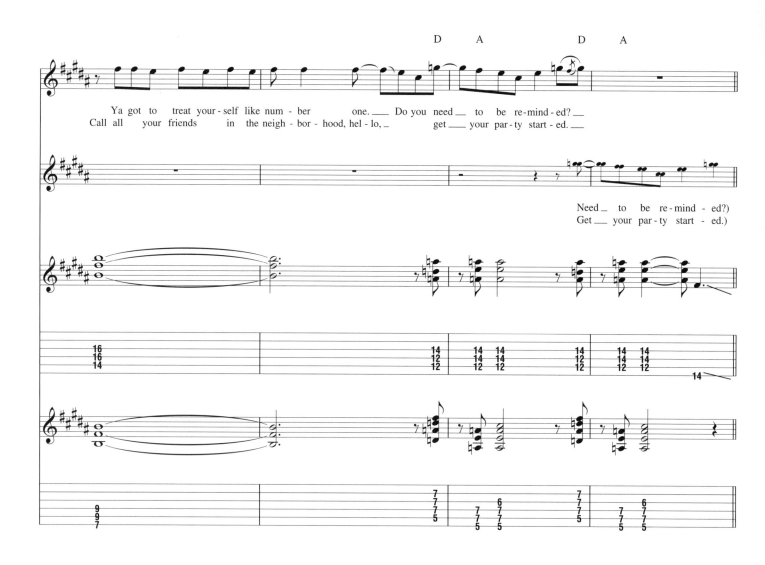

*Chord symbols reflect basic harmony.

Can't do it an - y oth - er way, ev - 'ry - bod -
And let's get row - dy with the girls and boys. ___ Time ___

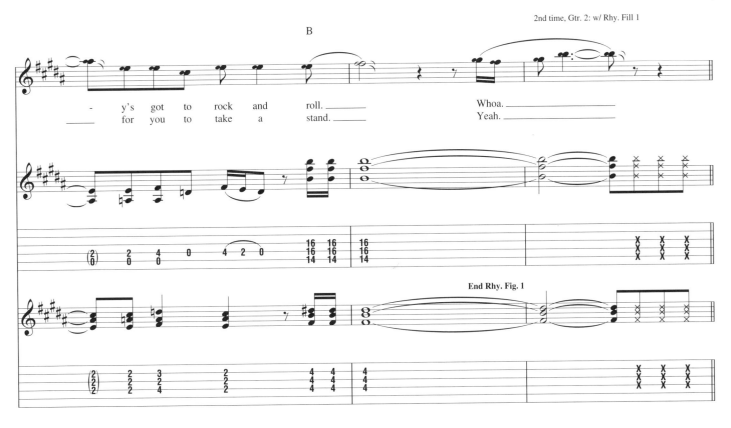

2nd time, Gtr. 2: w/ Rhy. Fill 1

- y's got to rock and roll. _____ Whoa. _____
for you to take a stand. _____ Yeah. _____

End Rhy. Fig. 1

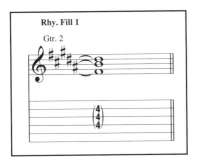

Rhy. Fill 1

Gtr. 2

All American Man

Words and Music by Paul Stanley and Sean Delaney

D5

Tune down 1/2 step:
(low to high) E♭-A♭-D♭-G♭-B♭-E♭

Intro
Moderately fast ♩ = 142

110

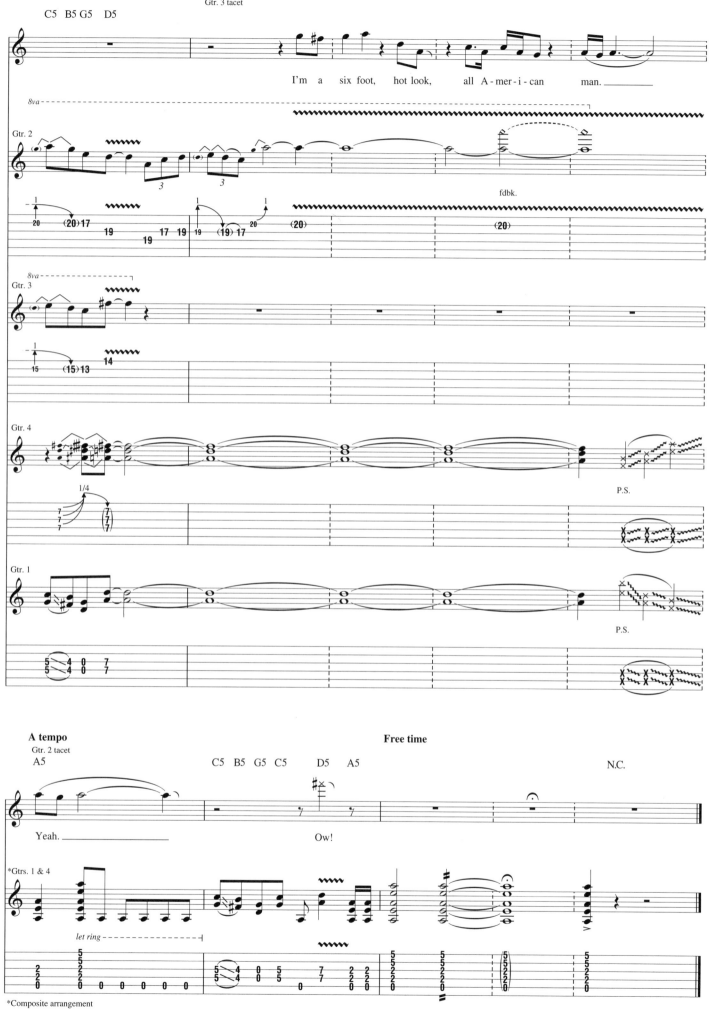

Rockin' in the U.S.A.

Words and Music by Gene Simmons

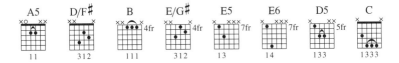

Tune down 1/2 step:
(low to high) Eb-Ab-Db-Gb-Bb-Eb

Intro

Moderately fast ♩ = 148

*Gtr. 2 (dist.)

*Two gtrs. arr. for one.

Gtr. 1 (dist.)

**Chord symbols reflect implied harmony.

***Slight P.H. 2nd time.

Verse

Gtr. 1: w/ Riff A (3 times)
2nd time, Gtr. 2: w/ Riff A1 (3 times)

fly-in' in a sev-en for-ty sev-en,   I'm pass-in' by the pear-ly gates. ___   And I'm
___ real-ly had the chance, ___ yeah,   there was plen-ty ro-mance.

Gtr. 2 tacet

Gtr. 1: w/ Riff B
2nd time, Gtr. 2: w/ Riff B1

com-in' real close to heav-en,   and my gui-tar ___ just can't ___ wait,
Eng-land too, ___ there was-n't much to do. ___   One thing I know is true, ___

Outro-Chorus

1st, 2nd & 3rd times, Gtrs. 1 & 2: w/ Rhy. Figs. 3 & 3A
Gtr. 3 tacet
4th time, Gtrs. 1 & 2: w/ Rhy. Figs. 3 & 3A (1st 6 meas.)

*Composite arrangement

Larger Than Life

Words and Music by Gene Simmons

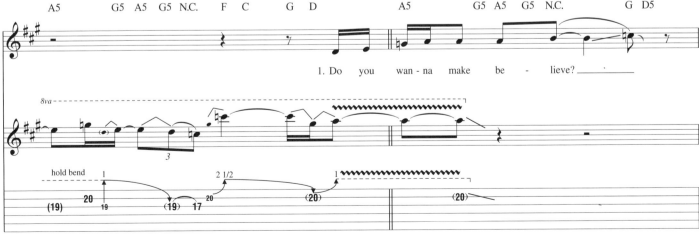

117

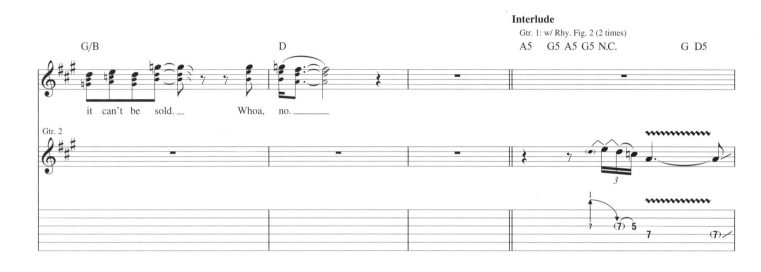

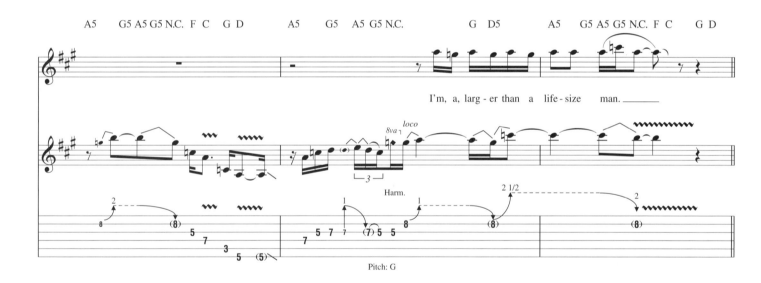

Outro-Chorus

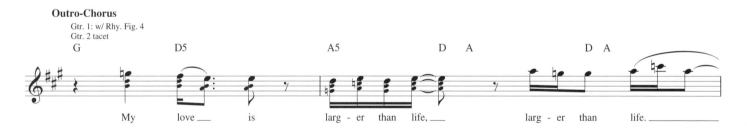

Rocket Ride

Words and Music by Ace Frehley and Sean Delaney

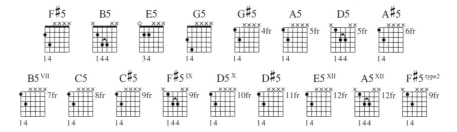

Tune down 1/2 step:
(low to high) Eb-Ab-Db-Gb-Bb-Eb

Intro
Moderately fast ♩ = 146

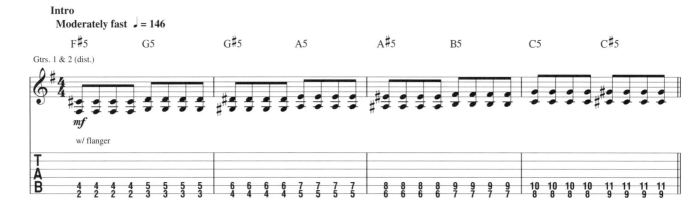

*Chord symbols reflect implied harmony.

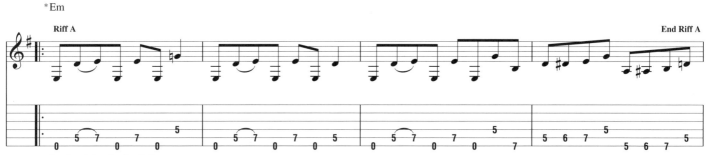

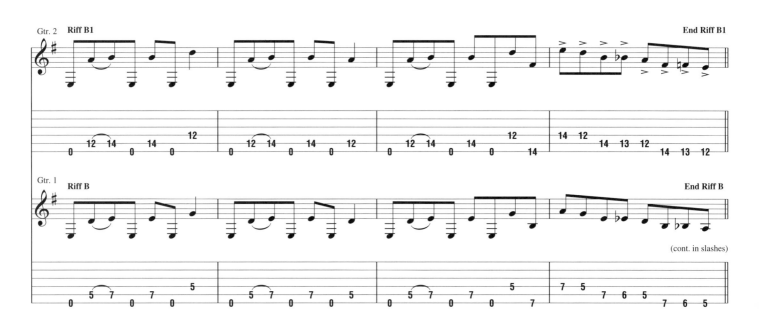

C'mon, grab a hold of my rocket!

Guitar Solo

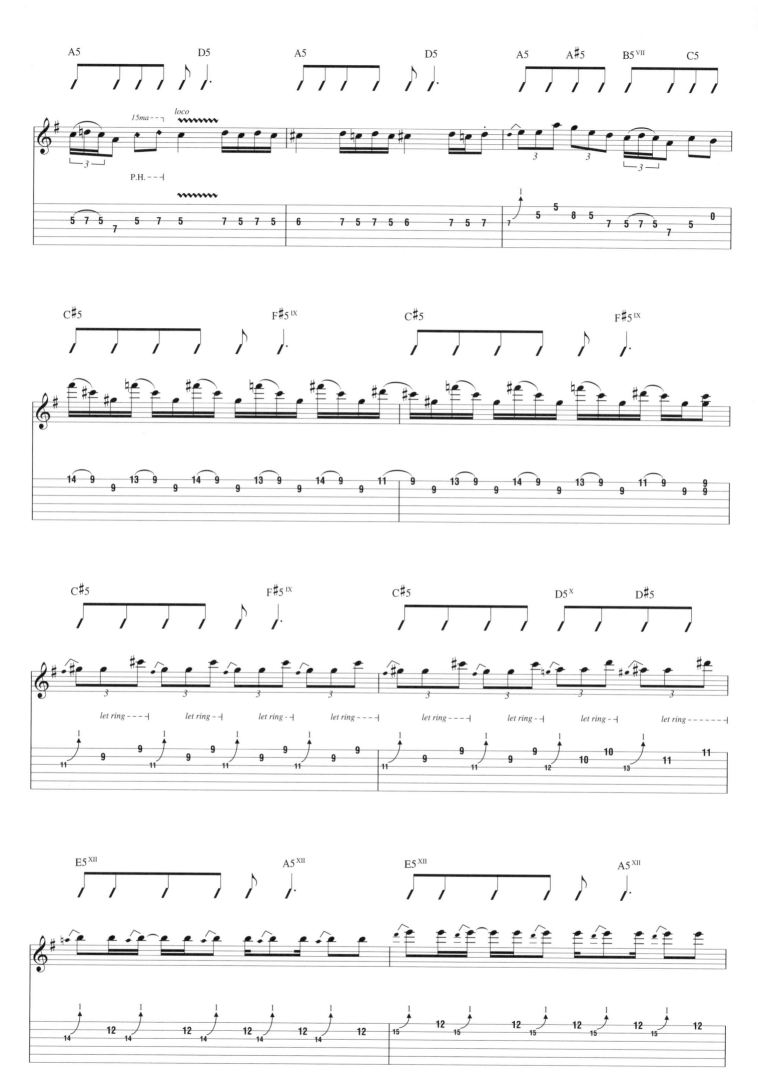

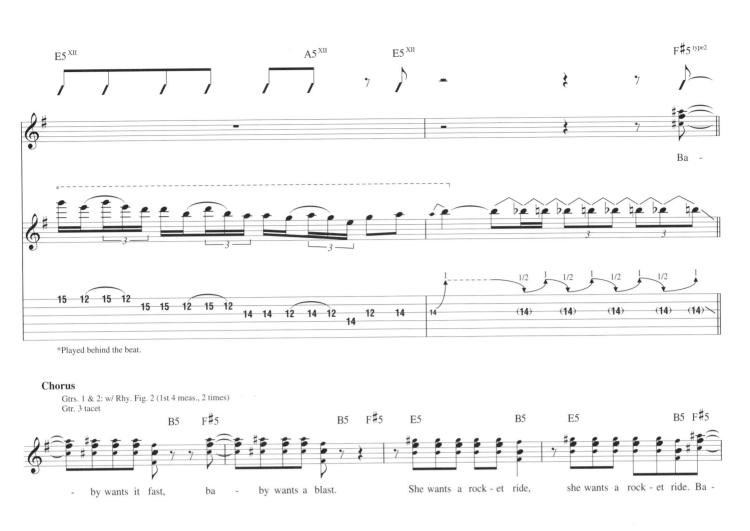

*Played behind the beat.

Chorus

Gtrs. 1 & 2: w/ Rhy. Fig. 2 (1st 4 meas., 2 times)
Gtr. 3 tacet

- by wants it fast, ba - by wants a blast. She wants a rock-et ride, she wants a rock-et ride. Ba -

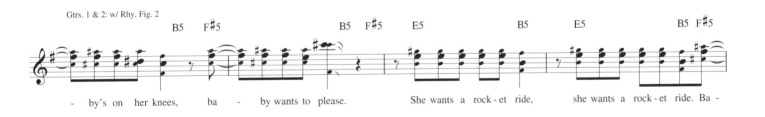

- by wants it fast, ba - by wants a blast. She wants a rock-et ride, she wants a rock-et ride. Ba -

Gtrs. 1 & 2: w/ Rhy. Fig. 2

- by's on her knees, ba - by wants to please. She wants a rock-et ride, she wants a rock-et ride. Ba -

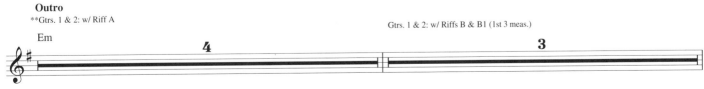

- by's on her knees, ba - by wants to please. She wants a rock-et ride, she wants a rock-et ride,

Outro

**Gtrs. 1 & 2: w/ Riff A

Gtrs. 1 & 2: w/ Riffs B & B1 (1st 3 meas.)

Em

**Flanger on

129

Any Way You Want It

Words and Music by Dave Clark

GUITAR NOTATION LEGEND

Guitar music can be notated three different ways: on a *musical staff*, in *tablature*, and in *rhythm slashes*.

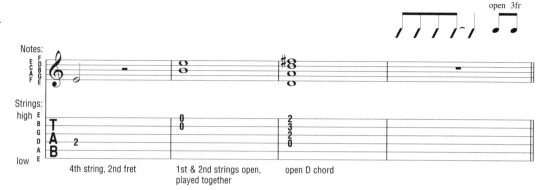

RHYTHM SLASHES are written above the staff. Strum chords in the rhythm indicated. Use the chord diagrams found at the top of the first page of the transcription for the appropriate chord voicings. Round noteheads indicate single notes.

THE MUSICAL STAFF shows pitches and rhythms and is divided by bar lines into measures. Pitches are named after the first seven letters of the alphabet.

TABLATURE graphically represents the guitar fingerboard. Each horizontal line represents a string, and each number represents a fret.

HALF-STEP BEND: Strike the note and bend up 1/2 step.

BEND AND RELEASE: Strike the note and bend up as indicated, then release back to the original note. Only the first note is struck.

HAMMER-ON: Strike the first (lower) note with one finger, then sound the higher note (on the same string) with another finger by fretting it without picking.

TRILL: Very rapidly alternate between the notes indicated by continuously hammering on and pulling off.

PICK SCRAPE: The edge of the pick is rubbed down (or up) the string, producing a scratchy sound.

TREMOLO PICKING: The note is picked as rapidly and continuously as possible.

WHOLE-STEP BEND: Strike the note and bend up one step.

PRE-BEND: Bend the note as indicated, then strike it.

PULL-OFF: Place both fingers on the notes to be sounded. Strike the first note and without picking, pull the finger off to sound the second (lower) note.

TAPPING: Hammer ("tap") the fret indicated with the pick-hand index or middle finger and pull off to the note fretted by the fret hand.

MUFFLED STRINGS: A percussive sound is produced by laying the fret hand across the string(s) without depressing, and striking them with the pick hand.

VIBRATO BAR DIVE AND RETURN: The pitch of the note or chord is dropped a specified number of steps (in rhythm), then returned to the original pitch.

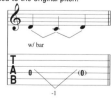

GRACE NOTE BEND: Strike the note and immediately bend up as indicated.

VIBRATO: The string is vibrated by rapidly bending and releasing the note with the fretting hand.

LEGATO SLIDE: Strike the first note and then slide the same fret-hand finger up or down to the second note. The second note is not struck.

NATURAL HARMONIC: Strike the note while the fret-hand lightly touches the string directly over the fret indicated.

PALM MUTING: The note is partially muted by the pick hand lightly touching the string(s) just before the bridge.

VIBRATO BAR SCOOP: Depress the bar just before striking the note, then quickly release the bar.

SLIGHT (MICROTONE) BEND: Strike the note and bend up 1/4 step.

WIDE VIBRATO: The pitch is varied to a greater degree by vibrating with the fretting hand.

SHIFT SLIDE: Same as legato slide, except the second note is struck.

PINCH HARMONIC: The note is fretted normally and a harmonic is produced by adding the edge of the thumb or the tip of the index finger of the pick hand to the normal pick attack.

RAKE: Drag the pick across the strings indicated with a single motion.

VIBRATO BAR DIP: Strike the note and then immediately drop a specified number of steps, then release back to the original pitch.

GUITAR RECORDED VERSIONS®

RECORDED VERSIONS GUITAR ®
AUTHENTIC TRANSCRIPTIONS WITH NOTES AND TABLATURE

Guitar Recorded Versions® are note-for-note transcriptions of guitar music taken directly off recordings. This series, one of the most popular in print today, features some of the greatest guitar players and groups from blues and rock to country and jazz.

Guitar Recorded Versions are transcribed by the best transcribers in the business. Every book contains notes and tablature. Visit www.halleonard.com for our complete selection.

00690016 The Will Ackerman Collection $19.95
00690501 Bryan Adams – Greatest Hits $19.95
00690002 Aerosmith – Big Ones $24.95
00692015 Aerosmith – Greatest Hits $22.95
00690603 Aerosmith – O Yeah! (Ultimate Hits) $24.95
00690147 Aerosmith – Rocks $19.95
00690146 Aerosmith – Toys in the Attic $19.99
00690139 Alice in Chains $19.95
00690178 Alice in Chains – Acoustic $19.95
00694865 Alice in Chains – Dirt $19.95
00660225 Alice in Chains – Facelift $19.95
00694925 Alice in Chains – Jar of Flies/Sap $19.95
00690387 Alice in Chains – Nothing Safe: Best of the Box $19.95
00690899 All That Remains – The Fall of Ideals $19.95
00690980 All That Remains – Overcome $22.99
00690812 All-American Rejects – Move Along $19.95
00690983 All-American Rejects – When the World Comes Down $22.99
00694932 Allman Brothers Band – Definitive Collection for Guitar Volume 1 ....$24.95
00694933 Allman Brothers Band – Definitive Collection for Guitar Volume 2 ....$24.95
00694934 Allman Brothers Band – Definitive Collection for Guitar Volume 3 ....$24.95
00690958 Duane Allman Guitar Anthology $24.99
00690945 Alter Bridge – Blackbird $22.99
00690755 Alter Bridge – One Day Remains $19.95
00690571 Trey Anastasio $19.95
00691013 The Answer – Everyday Demons $19.99
00690158 Chet Atkins – Almost Alone $19.95
00694876 Chet Atkins – Contemporary Styles $19.95
00694878 Chet Atkins – Vintage Fingerstyle $19.95
00690865 Atreyu – A Deathgrip on Yesterday $19.95
00690609 Audioslave $19.95
00690804 Audioslave – Out of Exile $19.95
00690884 Audioslave – Revelations $19.95
00690926 Avenged Sevenfold $22.95
00690820 Avenged Sevenfold – City of Evil $24.95
00694918 Randy Bachman Collection $22.95
00690366 Bad Company – Original Anthology – Book 1 ....$19.95
00690367 Bad Company – Original Anthology – Book 2 ....$19.95
00690503 Beach Boys – Very Best of $19.95
00694929 Beatles: 1962-1966 ....$24.95
00694930 Beatles: 1967-1970 ....$24.95
00690489 Beatles – 1 ....$24.99
00694880 Beatles – Abbey Road $19.95
00690110 Beatles – Book 1 (White Album) $19.95
00690111 Beatles – Book 2 (White Album) $19.95
00690902 Beatles – The Capitol Albums, Volume 1 ....$24.99
00694832 Beatles – For Acoustic Guitar $22.99
00690137 Beatles – A Hard Day's Night $16.95
00691031 Beatles – Help! $19.99
00690482 Beatles – Let It Be $17.95
00694891 Beatles – Revolver $19.95
00694914 Beatles – Rubber Soul $19.95
00694863 Beatles – Sgt. Pepper's Lonely Hearts Club Band $19.95
00690383 Beatles – Yellow Submarine $19.95
00690632 Beck – Sea Change $19.95
00694884 Best of George Benson $19.95
00692385 Chuck Berry $19.95
00690835 Billy Talent $19.95
00690879 Billy Talent II $19.95
00690149 Black Sabbath $14.95
00690901 Best of Black Sabbath $19.95
00691010 Black Sabbath – Heaven and Hell $22.99
00690148 Black Sabbath – Master of Reality $14.95
00690142 Black Sabbath – Paranoid $14.95
00692200 Black Sabbath – We Sold Our Soul for Rock 'N' Roll $19.95
00690674 blink-182 ....$19.95
00690389 blink-182 – Enema of the State $19.95
00690831 blink-182 – Greatest Hits $19.95
00690523 blink-182 – Take Off Your Pants and Jacket $19.95
00690028 Blue Oyster Cult – Cult Classics $19.95
00690851 James Blunt – Back to Bedlam $22.95
00690008 Bon Jovi – Cross Road $19.95
00690827 Bon Jovi – Have a Nice Day $22.95
00690913 Boston $19.95
00690932 Boston – Don't Look Back $19.99
00690829 Boston Guitar Collection $19.99
00690491 Best of David Bowie $19.95
00690583 Box Car Racer $19.95
00691023 Breaking Benjamin – Dear Agony $22.99
00690873 Breaking Benjamin – Phobia $19.95
00690764 Breaking Benjamin – We Are Not Alone $19.95
00690451 Jeff Buckley Collection $24.95
00690957 Bullet for My Valentine – Scream Aim Fire $19.95
00690678 Best of Kenny Burrell $19.95
00690564 The Calling – Camino Palmero $19.95
00690261 Carter Family Collection $19.95
00690043 Best of Cheap Trick $19.95
00690171 Chicago – The Definitive Guitar Collection $22.95
00691004 Chickenfoot $22.99
00691011 Chimaira Guitar Collection $24.99
00690567 Charlie Christian – The Definitive Collection $19.95
00690590 Eric Clapton – Anthology $29.95
00692391 Best of Eric Clapton – 2nd Edition $22.95
00690936 Eric Clapton – Complete Clapton $29.99
00690074 Eric Clapton – Cream of Clapton $24.95
00690247 Eric Clapton – 461 Ocean Boulevard $19.99
00690010 Eric Clapton – From the Cradle $19.95
00690716 Eric Clapton – Me and Mr. Johnson $19.95
00694873 Eric Clapton – Timepieces $19.95
00694869 Eric Clapton – Unplugged $22.95
00690415 Clapton Chronicles – Best of Eric Clapton $18.95
00694896 John Mayall/Eric Clapton – Bluesbreakers $19.95
00690162 Best of the Clash $19.95
00690828 Coheed & Cambria – Good Apollo I'm Burning Star, IV, Vol. 1: From Fear Through the Eyes of Madness $19.95
00690940 Coheed and Cambria – No World for Tomorrow $19.95
00690494 Coldplay – Parachutes $19.95
00690593 Coldplay – A Rush of Blood to the Head $19.95
00690906 Coldplay – The Singles & B-Sides $24.95
00690962 Coldplay – Viva La Vida $19.95
00690806 Coldplay – X & Y $19.95
00690855 Best of Collective Soul $19.95
00690928 Chris Cornell – Carry On $19.95
00694940 Counting Crows – August & Everything After $19.95
00690405 Counting Crows – This Desert Life $19.95
00694840 Cream – Disraeli Gears $19.95
00690285 Cream – Those Were the Days $17.95
00690819 Best of Creedence Clearwater Revival $22.95
00690648 The Very Best of Jim Croce $19.95
00690572 Steve Cropper – Soul Man $19.95
00690613 Best of Crosby, Stills & Nash $22.95
00690777 Crossfade $19.95
00699521 The Cure – Greatest Hits $24.95
00690637 Best of Dick Dale $19.95
00690941 Dashboard Confessional – The Shade of Poison Trees $19.95
00690892 Daughtry $19.95
00690822 Best of Alex De Grassi $19.95
00690967 Death Cab for Cutie – Narrow Stairs $22.99
00690289 Best of Deep Purple $17.95
00690288 Deep Purple – Machine Head $17.99
00690784 Best of Def Leppard $19.95
00694831 Derek and the Dominos – Layla & Other Assorted Love Songs $22.95
00692240 Bo Diddley – Guitar Solos by Fred Sokolow $19.99
00690384 Best of Ani DiFranco $19.95
00690322 Ani DiFranco – Little Plastic Castle $19.95
00690380 Ani DiFranco – Up Up Up Up Up Up $19.95
00690979 Best of Dinosaur Jr. $19.99
00690833 Private Investigations – Best of Dire Straits and Mark Knopfler $24.95
00695382 Very Best of Dire Straits – Sultans of Swing $22.95
00690347 The Doors – Anthology $22.95
00690348 The Doors – Essential Guitar Collection $16.95
00690915 Dragonforce – Inhuman Rampage $29.99
00690250 Best of Duane Eddy $16.95
00690533 Electric Light Orchestra Guitar Collection $19.95
00690909 Best of Tommy Emmanuel $19.95
00690555 Best of Melissa Etheridge $19.95
00690496 Best of Everclear $19.95
00690515 Extreme II – Pornograffitti $19.95
00690982 Fall Out Boy – Folie à Deux $22.99
00690810 Fall Out Boy – From Under the Cork Tree $19.95
00690897 Fall Out Boy – Infinity on High $22.95
00691009 Five Finger Death Punch $19.99
00690664 Best of Fleetwood Mac $19.95
00690870 Flyleaf $19.95
00690257 John Fogerty – Blue Moon Swamp $19.95
00690931 Foo Fighters – Echoes, Silence, Patience & Grace $19.95
00690235 Foo Fighters – The Colour and the Shape $19.95
00690808 Foo Fighters – In Your Honor $19.95
00690595 Foo Fighters – One by One $19.95
00690394 Foo Fighters – There Is Nothing Left to Lose $19.95
00690805 Best of Robben Ford $19.95
00690842 Best of Peter Frampton $19.95
00690734 Franz Ferdinand $19.95
00694920 Best of Free $19.95
00690222 G3 Live – Joe Satriani, Steve Vai, and Eric Johnson $22.95
00694807 Danny Gatton – 88 Elmira St $19.95
00690438 Genesis Guitar Anthology $19.95
00690753 Best of Godsmack $19.95
00120167 Godsmack $19.95
00690848 Godsmack – IV $19.95
00690338 Goo Goo Dolls – Dizzy Up the Girl $19.95
00690576 Goo Goo Dolls – Gutterflower $19.95
00690927 Patty Griffin – Children Running Through $19.95
00690591 Patty Griffin – Guitar Collection $19.95
00690978 Guns N' Roses – Chinese Democracy $24.99
00691027 Buddy Guy Anthology $24.99
00694854 Buddy Guy – Damn Right, I've Got the Blues $19.95
00690697 Best of Jim Hall $19.95
00690840 Ben Harper – Both Sides of the Gun $19.95
00690987 Ben Harper and Relentless7 – White Lies for Dark Times $22.99
00694798 George Harrison Anthology $19.95
00690778 Hawk Nelson – Letters to the President $19.95
00690841 Scott Henderson – Blues Guitar Collection $19.95
00692930 Jimi Hendrix – Are You Experienced? $24.95
00692931 Jimi Hendrix – Axis: Bold As Love $22.95
00690304 Jimi Hendrix – Band of Gypsys $24.99
00690321 Jimi Hendrix – BBC Sessions $22.95
00690608 Jimi Hendrix – Blue Wild Angel $24.95
00694944 Jimi Hendrix – Blues $24.95
00692932 Jimi Hendrix – Electric Ladyland $24.95
00690602 Jimi Hendrix – Smash Hits $24.99
00691033 Jimi Hendrix – Valleys of Neptune $22.99
00690017 Jimi Hendrix – Woodstock $24.95
00690843 H.I.M. – Dark Light $19.95
00690869 Hinder – Extreme Behavior $19.95
00660029 Buddy Holly $19.95
00690793 John Lee Hooker Anthology $24.99
00660169 John Lee Hooker – A Blues Legend $19.95
00694905 Howlin' Wolf $19.95
00690692 Very Best of Billy Idol $19.95
00690688 Incubus – A Crow Left of the Murder $19.95
00690544 Incubus – Morningview $19.95
00690136 Indigo Girls – 1200 Curfews $22.95
00690790 Iron Maiden Anthology $24.99
00690887 Iron Maiden – A Matter of Life and Death $24.95
00690730 Alan Jackson – Guitar Collection $19.95
00694938 Elmore James – Master Electric Slide Guitar $19.95
00690652 Best of Jane's Addiction $19.95
00690721 Jet – Get Born $19.95
00690684 Jethro Tull – Aqualung $19.95
00690693 Jethro Tull Guitar Anthology $19.95
00690647 Best of Jewel $19.95
00690898 John 5 – The Devil Knows My Name $22.95
00690959 John 5 – Requiem $22.95
00690814 John 5 – Songs for Sanity $19.95
00690751 John 5 – Vertigo $19.95
00694912 Eric Johnson – Ah Via Musicom $19.95